LIVING ON THE THIRD RIVER

BY
CRAIG HILL

FAMILY FOUNDATIONS INTERNATIONAL
LITTLETON, COLORADO
WWW.FAMILYFOUNDATIONS.COM

Family Foundations International
P.O. Box 320
Littleton, Colorado 80160
www.familyfoundations.com

Original Cover design by
Counterpoint Design
Modified Cover design by
Jason Dudley

Printed in the United States of America

Scripture quotations are taken from:
The New King James Bible, Thomas Nelson Publishers, 1982; The Amplified Bible, Zondervan Bible Publishers, 1965, 12th Printing, 1975.

The characters in many of the examples cited in this book are real life people whom the authors have known. For their privacy, however, their names and some of the insignificant details have been altered. Alternatively, some incidents described are not sequential events, but are composites of several incidents; nevertheless, they reflect very real situations.

First Edition 2002
Second Edition 2006
Third Edition 2010

TABLE OF CONTENTS

chapter 1
ON WHICH RIVER DO YOU LIVE?

While teaching in Africa, the Lord gave me a picture depicting the management of financial resource. I saw a huge snowfield in the mountains with a virtually infinite supply of water. There were three rivers emanating from this snowfield. On the first river, lives a man whose experience of life is such that he never quite had enough water. Life experience has confirmed that to him. So, what does he do with the water coming down the river? He builds a dam in the river, and collects all the water that he possibly can. No water is ever able to flow downstream for others to use. This man's view of water only includes that which is available to him in his lake. Therefore, he must conserve water, and he must be very careful because there is never enough coming down for him.

If the flow of water is ever increased in his river, he will simply store it and increase the size of his lake. His perception is that the bigger lake he has, the more secure he is for the future.

A second river also flows down from the snowfield. The man who lives along this river has life experience that tells him there is usually plenty of water to meet his needs, so there is no need to build a dam in the river. However, there is never quite enough water to really meet all of his desires for water usage.

Thus, he uses all the water he can and lets a very small amount flow downstream for others to use. However, most of the water coming down the river is consumed by his ever-expanding needs/desires, so not much is left to flow downstream. This man's view of water is that there is more water available upstream, but its volume and rate of flow is quite limited. Therefore, he uses all he can as it flows down through his property.

If the flow of water is increased in this river, this family will inevitably find new uses for water. This man will build a swimming pool for his children. If water flow still increases, he will build a water park and install a series of beautiful fountains on his property. No matter how much water comes down the river, there is never quite enough for him to really do everything he would like to do with water.

Finally, there is a third river and a man who lives along this river. His experience of life is that there is so much water up there in that snowfield that no one could ever use all the water coming down the river. Because of his understanding, this man begins digging canals to outlying areas to help water the fields of others who do not live near a river. He empties as much water as he can out through the canals he has dug and there still seems to be more water flowing down the river than he can possibly use, so most of it still flows downstream for others to use.

Each year this man digs a few new canals out to his neighbors, who need water. In the next year, he has a plan for another three canals. Then the following year, he is hoping to dig five new canals that can go out even further from this river. It seems like no matter how many canals he digs, there is just more water that keeps coming down the river. In fact, this man is thinking all the time about how he can hire some more men with more bulldozers to help dig canals faster to get water out to all the other farms that are far from the river. This man's experience of life is that he just cannot use up all that water coming down the river.

If the flow of water is increased in this river, the man living along this river will simply dig more canals to get more and more water out to help others.

On which river do you live?

chapter 2
DOES THE BIBLE TALK ABOUT MONEY

D oes God have anything to say about money in the Bible?" Many people consider the Bible to be a book pertaining to spirituality, but not to such mundane matters as personal management of money. Most people would be shocked to discover that the New Testament contains nearly ten times as many verses regarding money and finances as it does regarding salvation and faith. **The New Testament actually contains <u>215</u> verses pertaining to faith, <u>218</u> verses pertaining to salvation, and <u>2,084</u> verses dealing with the stewardship of and accountability for money and finance. Sixteen of Jesus' thirty-eight parables deal with money.**

The question comes to mind, "Why?" Was Jesus a money-grubber? Did He come to earth to collect money to support His ministry? No, of course not! Jesus was not after peoples' money. He was after their hearts. He told us in Matthew 6:21, "Where your treasure is there shall your heart be also". Jesus simply found that many people put an awful lot of treasure in their money. He found that if He could capture their money, He could capture their hearts. The same is true today. Jesus is not after your money. He is after your heart. **How we relate to money is simply indicative of the condition of our hearts.**

I ran across a recent statistic citing the fact that 80% of North American Christian homes have some type of financial distress, ranging from mild to serious. A primary issue cited in 50% of divorces in America today has to do with finances. Relationship as a couple has broken down due to either the mismanagement of finances, the lack of agreement over the usage of finances, or the mishandling of debt. In reality, the life of every single person is also greatly impacted by his or her relationship to finances. Consequently, God indeed has much to say to us about finances, and He has given us His Word to instruct us.

MATTHEW 6

24 No one can serve two masters; for either he will hate the one and love the other, or else he will be loyal to the one and despise the other. You cannot serve God and Mammon.

This peculiar saying spoken by Jesus Christ about two thousand years ago has been a source of guilt, controversy, and contention for believers in Jesus for centuries. What did Jesus mean by saying, "You cannot serve God and Mammon"? What *is* "Mammon, anyway?" The word "Mammon" is frequently used as if it were just another word for money. Is this correct? Some English translations of the Bible even substitute the word money for the word Mammon used in the above-quoted passage. Does this word have another meaning of which we are unaware? If I truly want to serve God, does this mean that I should then avoid all contact with, or possession of,

6

money? These are all questions, which have passed through the minds of most readers of the New Testament.

Let us begin by talking about the meaning of the above-quoted passage in Matthew 6. To what is Jesus referring when He uses the word "Mammon?" Firstly, it is important to see that whatever Mammon is, Jesus places it in a position that is diametrically opposed to God. It is anti-God. Whatever Mammon is competes with God to be served. When He said that the two, God and Mammon, could not both be served, Jesus was not speaking about a prohibition against such, but rather an impossibility of doing such. Jesus was not stating, "It would be wrong to try to serve both God and Mammon", but rather, "It is impossible to serve both God and Mammon." God and Mammon are opposites, and thus cannot both be served at the same time. Serving one categorically precludes serving the other. Thus, either God or Mammon can only be served exclusively. In order to truly serve God, one must totally renounce Mammon and have nothing at all to do with it.

Now, if "Mammon" is synonymous with "money", then the obvious conclusion is that the Christian believer should totally renounce and have nothing to do with money. People in past centuries, and some even today have believed this and thus have taken a vow of poverty and avoided all contact with money in an attempt to be wholly devoted to God. However, even taking a vow of poverty does not necessarily free one from greed or the fear of lack of provision. Thus, it is evident that Jesus' reference to Mammon is not synonymous with money.

I was interested to discover that Ron Smith, the founder of the Youth with a Mission School of Biblical

Studies, had done some research into the Canaanite culture at the time of Jesus. Ron had been interested enough to look into the origin of the word "mammon" and had discovered that the Philistines at that time worshiped and prayed to a false god of finance called in Aramaic, "Mammon." Thus, it is very likely that Jesus was referring to this idolatrous god of the Philistines called Mammon when He used this phrase in Matthew 6, rather than to money itself.

Frequently throughout their history, the Israelites had wanted to worship both the gods of the peoples in whose land they had dwelt as well as Jehovah God. Joshua had called the people to forsake trying to serve both the false gods of the Amorites and Jehovah, but rather to choose whom they would serve, for to serve both was a choice against Jehovah. (Joshua 24:15-28). It seems that Jesus here in Matthew 6 is telling His disciples that they cannot serve both the false Philistine god of finance, Mammon, and Jehovah God. They must choose. We would have readily understood had Jesus said, "You cannot serve God and Baal," or "God and Dagon", or today, "God and Buddha". We have heard of these other false gods. Most people, however, have been unfamiliar with Mammon.

What is the nature of these false gods that were worshipped by various Canaanite peoples? Were these just human-created idols? I do not think so. It seems that each of these idolatrous gods were actually demonic princes in Satan's kingdom, who were able to deceive peoples into worshipping them. Thus, Baal, Chemosh, Molech, Dagon, Mammon, etc. were not just human-created idols, but rather were demonic spirits, worshipped by people. Are these spirits still alive and operative today? They most certainly are! Thus the demonic spirit behind money, Mammon, is still operative and demanding worship,

8

influence, and control of peoples' lives to love and trust money today even as it was in the days of Jesus' life on earth.

When Jesus states that you cannot serve both God and Mammon, it appears that He is contrasting two spiritual entities. In reality, money is impotent and has no power. <u>God has power</u>. <u>The spirit of Mammon has power</u>. <u>Money has no power</u>. Thus, the true power behind financial provision in your life will be either God or the spirit of Mammon, depending on whom you choose to serve. Most people, including Christians falsely believe that the real power is in money. **Therefore, until you realize the impotence of money, you will never be free from its pursuit, nor from the influence and dominion of the spirit behind it.**

chapter 3
INTENT OF THE SPIRIT OF MAMMON

Let us consider the purpose of this demonic entity called Mammon. Firstly, we know that any spirit operative in Satan's kingdom desires to turn the hearts of people away from God. I believe that the primary purpose of the spirit of Mammon is to obtain from people their worship, love, loyalty, service and fear. Mammon loves to hear us refer to money as the "Almighty Dollar". In Matthew 6:24 and Luke 16:13, Jesus identifies the conflict of love, loyalty and service between God and Mammon. He says that if you love one, you will hate the other. If you are loyal to one, you will despise the other, and if you serve one, you cannot serve the other. So the purpose of Mammon is to get you to be loyal to, love and serve him, so that by default you will hate, despise, and not serve God. As Joshua called the children of Israel to attention: "Choose this day Whom you will serve" (Joshua 24), so the Lord poses the same question to us today.

As with all demonic entities, the primary assault is not direct, but rather operates in a cloaked manner through deception. If Mammon were to directly appear to any Christian or even unbeliever, reveal his identity and demand loyalty, love and service, very few would voluntarily submit to him. Thus, the primary tactic of Mammon is to entice people to serve him without realizing that they are doing so. He does this through propagating lies that are widely believed in the heart by most people to be truth. I believe that <u>the paramount lie spread by the spirit of Mammon is that money contains inherent power.</u> Mammon entices people to ascribe sacred power to money. A person who has much money is thought to be very powerful, while a person with little money is impotent. Value is ascribed to people based on net worth of money. This fact is also true about currency in a country. When a country's money is stable, we consider the country powerful.

Mammon entices people to place disproportionate value on money. When people believe that money has power, they are tempted to love money. This love of money then gives rise to many other forms of wickedness.

1 TIMOTHY 6

10 For the love of money is a root of all kinds of evil, for some have strayed from the faith in their greediness, and pierced themselves through with many sorrows.

Christians who believe the lie that money has power allow their travel and movements to be governed by money, rather than by God. Such ones fear the lack of money, consult their checkbook rather than God in their giving of offerings, and busy themselves with all sorts of schemes promising to deliver money. The truth is that money has no power. It is simply an amoral, impotent object, to which the spirit of Mammon ascribes great power and through which he attempts to control the lives of people.

A corollary lie, believed by many, is that the source of one's provision is his/her employer, spouse, investments, or other channel through which money is supplied. The truth, of course, is that the power is in God, not money, and that He is the source of provision. Thus, for the believer, there is a conflict of service and love. If one loves money, then by default he does not love God. If one empowers money to govern choices in her life, she has without realizing it, empowered the spirit of Mammon to rule her life. God may speak to such a person to go to a certain place, give to a certain ministry, or do a certain thing and she will say to God, "I can't, because I don't have enough money". Now God is not the source, but money is the source. If you simply ask most people the question, "For what purpose do you work?" they will answer, "I am working for money". Money thus is the goal, the master, or the real source of power. Money was never intended to be my master, but rather to be my servant. **I am not to work for money, but rather money is supposed to work for me to accomplish God's purposes.**

The key issue here is, "Who is my source?" The spirit of Mammon will continually attempt to convince us that the real power for life is in money and that the channel through which it comes is my source. Thus, if I have accepted in my heart that my employer or, my husband, my investments, my business or the economy is my source, without realizing it, I have become a slave to the spirit of Mammon.

The master/slave relationship is thus perverted. When God is my source, then money becomes my slave to be pressed into service for the Kingdom of God. A slave is accountable to his master. We should direct money's activity and know where it is at all times. However, when money is my source, then I become the slave of Mammon doing whatever I perceive is necessary to get money. In other words, the end and means are reversed. Money should rightly be the means by which to serve God, Who is the end or the goal. When money is empowered as a source of life then God becomes the means by which Christians hope to get money. This is many times a very subtle distinction.

I have often been present in churches in which an offering is being received, and I have felt my spirit reacting negatively to something about how the offering was being taken. For years, I could not identify the problem, but I just felt inside that something was wrong. Finally, I was able in recent years to identify that the problem is that the offering was being motivated by the spirit of Mammon rather than by the Spirit of God. The end and means had been reversed. <u>Rather than using money to serve God, people were being encouraged to use God to get money</u>.

The offering was taken something like this. (We often speak of "taking an offering," while "receiving an offering" would embody more of a Kingdom mentality.) Lack of money was first identified as a prevailing need for many people. Next, it was brought out in scripture that lack and poverty were not God's will. The biblical principle of sowing and reaping was then presented from Mark 4 or other such passages. The person taking the offering would then let people know that the way to get their needs met was to sow seed (money) into the offering and that God would then return 30, 60 or 100 fold. Now what is wrong with this?

It is true that poverty and lack are not God's will for His people. He does want to provide for His people and it is His will to bless people. Sowing and reaping is a biblical principle that does indeed apply to money. God does want to multiply financial seed many-fold. So, what is the problem? The problem, of course, is the reversal of the master/slave, end/means relationship. This approach empowers money as the goal. "*You* don't have enough money. We are going to use God and God's principles to get you money. When you have money, then you will be OK." NO! God is not the servant to get you money. Money is your servant to expand the Kingdom. God is your Master. You are His steward called to manage money under His direction.

The truth then is that God is meant to be the master and money is meant to be our slave to expand the Kingdom of God. We are to use money to serve God, not use God to get money. If God is truly my source, then my employer, investments, bank account, or spouse is merely the channel through whom my current provision comes from God. Thus if I receive news that my job will terminate or the economy fails, I am not terrorized by fear of lack of provision, as the source (God) is still the same. He is simply changing the channel of my provision. **If God is my source, then money becomes my slave with which to serve the Kingdom. If money is my source, then God will not be my slave to get me money.** Thus, God has power and Mammon has power, but money has no power. Money will be either my slave or my master depending on whether I am serving God or the spirit of Mammon.

A good friend of mine, Earl Pitts, first helped me to understand this concept. Earl had worked for the IBM Corporation for 19 years and had come to the realization that IBM was not his source. He could not serve (be in the employment of) two masters. He had to settle the issue that God was his source (employer) and that God had designated him to give his time to IBM and had delegated IBM to pay his salary. What a place of peace! Later, when the Lord called Earl to leave IBM and join a Christian missions group, he was able to do so without fear of lack of provision. He realized that God was still his source and that He had ways to flow money to him through different channels.

chapter 4
INFLUENCE OF THE
SPIRIT OF MAMMON

Most people do not recognize the influence of the spirit of Mammon on their lives. My friend Earl first helped me identify ten clear symptoms of the influence of the spirit of Mammon in a person's life. Identification of the influence of this spirit is the first step to freedom from it. Listed in the following pages are those ten symptoms.

1. **Worry and anxiety over money.**

Many people carry much anxiety and fear over money. Rich people have the fear of loosing money, while poor people have the fear of never having enough money. In either case fear, worry and anxiety dominate a person's emotions.

2. **Money mismanagement.** "I don't know where it went."

Many Christians have no system of record keeping for their personal finances. Because of this, they have no financial accountability in their lives, even to themselves.

Such people could not even tell you the regular monthly amount necessary for their provision.

3. **Consistent financial lack.** "I don't ever have enough money." Too much month left at the end of the money.

This problem seems to afflict both the rich and the poor alike. When I do not see myself as a manager of finances, accountable before God, then I will have no record keeping and no plan. This results in spending patterns that consistently exceed available resource. The deception of consumer debt then becomes very attractive as a short-term solution for financial lack.

4. **"I can't afford it" mentality.**

As good stewards, we have to answer the question "how much is enough?" The Mammon spirit does not want us to answer that question. When we seek God as to what should be in our budget in the Needs and Wants area, and we obey what He tells us, then the "I can't afford it" mentality is a non-issue. If you have truly sought the Lord regarding His will and timing for you to have a particular item, then it should be included in your budget. When you follow this strategy, the temptation from advertising to create need in your heart and mind is defeated.

5. **Impulse buying.** Inability to resist the desire to purchase.

Many times a person will come home with a new purchase and the marriage partner will exclaim, "Why did you buy that? What do we need it for?" The answer will come, "I don't know, but I got a deal. It was cheap." Many people purchase all sorts of things that they really do not need or even want simply because it was cheap. This is a pattern established in the lives of many people who have not yet learned to be a manager of resources and to allow the Holy Spirit to be the master. The secret is to always shop with a purpose. Make sure to go with a list, including items to be purchased and/or names of people you want to bless!

6. **Stinginess.** This is exemplified by a fear of giving.

Some people have more fear of letting go of money than Scrooge does at Christmas time. Fear of tithing or regular giving is always a symptom of a strong yielding to the spirit of Mammon. Stinginess is simply a fear that I will not have enough money to meet my own needs. This fear again afflicts both the rich and the poor

7. **Greed.** This is an inordinate desire to acquire or possess.

Some people mix the definitions of covetousness and greed. What is the difference? Covetousness has to do with desiring after something that you do not have, while greed is the desire for more of what you already have. In Luke 12:16-20 Jesus tells us a story of a rich man who was continually building barns to contain more of his crops and goods. In the end, God called him a fool and told him that his trust in his possessions and not in God would cost him his soul. If you ask a wealthy man who has never answered the question "How much is enough?" he will answer you, "Just a little bit more".

8. **Discontentment**.

PHILIPPIANS 4

11 Not that I am implying that I was in any personal want, for I have learned how to be content (satisfied to the point where I am not disturbed or disquieted) in whatever state I am.

12 I know how to be abased and live humbly in straitened circumstances, and I know also how to enjoy plenty and live in abundance. I have learned in any and all circumstances, the secret of facing every situation, whether well-fed or going hungry, having a sufficiency and to spare or going without and being in want.

13 I have the strength for all things in Christ Who empowers me. (Amplified)

Some people can identify with Paul and say that they know what it is to be in want. However, the key to the verses is that Paul knew HOW to live in both situations. He "knows how" to have life with much or little. When we look at Paul's circumstances, we find that the times when he had little were when God told him to give away what he had. Knowing how to live with having little or much was to not be controlled by the spirit of Mammon. The key is to continue to look to God as a source in every situation and to never allow yourself to become discontent because of your circumstances.

9. **Bondage to debt.** (Psalm 7:15; 37:21)

Psalm 7

15 He made a pit and dug it out, and has fallen into the ditch which he made. (NKJV)

Psalm 37

21 The wicked borrows and does not repay, But the righteous shows mercy and gives. (NKJV)

There is a spirit behind personal debt, which couples itself with Mammon and will hinder the flow of finances in one's life. Debt is one of the chief mechanisms used by the spirit of Mammon to keep people in bondage to itself. When the spirit of Mammon is ruling in a person's life, he or she is frequently placed in financial slavery through the weight of interest owed on debt. People in bondage to the spirit of Mammon are often not able to discipline themselves to delay the personal gratification of the immediate purchase of desired items. Unplanned consumer debt is always a very strong indicator of the lordship of the spirit of Mammon in a person's life. We must learn how to manage our personal debt to get out of it and stay out of it

10. **Exaggerated emphasis on money and an overestimate of its true power.**

Often one can hear this emphasis in the language people use. When you listen to some people talk, most of what they are talking about has to do with money. They are very impressed by others who have a lot of money. They are constantly talking about how they might make more money. There is continually a strong emphasis in their conversation on pursuing money. **However, God's plan was for money to pursue us.** We are not meant to be working to make money, but rather to be looking for ways to release money and make it work for us. If money is the determining factor for you to do something, then you are for sale. **If you are for sale, the devil will find your price.**

If you have recognized one or more of these symptoms of the Mammon spirit's influence in your life, let us stop and pray right now. I want to lead you to pray to break the power of this spirit's influence and to tear down the strongholds that may have arisen in your mind. Pray this prayer with me.

"Heavenly Father, thank You for revealing to us (me) the influence that the spirit of Mammon has had in our (my) life. Lord, we (I) renounce the allegiance that this spirit has had in our (my) heart(s). We (I) purposefully break the power of the spirit of Mammon in our lives (my life) and over our (my) finances. We (I) revoke today any authority that we (I) have given Mammon, and we (I) give that authority to Jesus Christ alone. Lord, forgive us (me) for focusing on money instead of on You. We (I) ask you, Lord to renew our (my) mind(s) to the truth that You are the source of our (my) provision, and that anything we (I) receive is a gift from You. We (I) trust You to meet our (my) financial needs because You love us (me). Amen."

chapter 5
SPARROW FAITH

How a Christian relates to money is an indicator of his/her understanding of God's grace. The basic operative principle in God's economy is giving and receiving, while the basic operative principle in the world system is buying and selling. Giving and receiving is a unilateral manifestation of grace. When you give, you expect nothing in return. The acts of buying and selling demand an exchange. So when I take that which was designed by man for buying and selling, namely money, and freely give it with no expectation of return, I have introduced money to grace. In doing so, I have profaned the sacred properties ascribed to money and have declared to the spiritual and natural realm that Mammon is not my source.

Now when a Christian gives in an offering with an expectation of return in order to get his/her needs met, he/she is not understanding God's grace. If I have heard it once, I have heard it taught a hundred times that if you are experiencing financial lack, the way to get your needs met is by financial sowing and reaping. This is wrong, wrong, wrong, wrong, wrong. This understanding nullifies the grace of God, places one back in the world system of exchange and submits one's heart to be governed by the spirit of Mammon while thinking one is serving God. Jesus taught further in the Matthew 6 passage specifically against this idea of sowing and reaping to meet one's needs.

MATTHEW 6

24 No one can serve two masters; for either he will hate the one and love the other, or else he will be loyal to the one and despise the other. You cannot serve God and Mammon.

25 Therefore I say to you, do not worry about your life, what you will eat or what you will drink; nor about your body, what you will put on. Is not life more than food and the body more than clothing?

26 Look at the birds of the air, for they neither sow nor reap nor gather into barns; yet your Heavenly Father feeds them. Are you not of more value than they? Which of you by worrying can add one cubit to his stature? So why do you worry about clothing? Consider the lilies of the field, how they grow: they neither toil nor spin; and yet I say to you that even Solomon in all his glory was not arrayed like one of these. (NKJV)

Here we see Jesus introducing His disciples to grace, by breaking the lie that God through sowing and reaping will meet human needs. Jesus is making the point that God provides the basic needs of sparrows and lilies without their sowing or reaping or toiling or spinning. In other words, their provision is not dependent upon their works. Birds and flowers are cared for by God simply because He values them. Jesus then makes the point that you as a person are of much greater value to God than birds and flowers. Thus, Jesus teaches that basic provision for life is made by your Heavenly Father just because He loves you. This is what I have come to call "Sparrow Faith". Sparrow Faith is the initial foundation upon which all other financial operations in the Kingdom of God must be based. Without the foundation of Sparrow Faith, a basic trust that God will provide for my needs because He loves me, subsequent biblical principles of finance are easily distorted by the spirit of Mammon and used to confuse people.

You may ask, "Are you saying that financial sowing and reaping with an expectation of return is wrong?" No, not at all! Sowing and reaping is a correct biblical principle, but not to be used for getting ones needs met. The way this principle is frequently taught nullifies God's grace and makes the meeting of your needs dependent upon your works, not upon God's love.

Sparrow Faith is the foundational corner stone of Christian financial structure. This is an absolute trust, confidence, and leaning of one's entire personality upon God's love and provision. Thus, the provision that I now receive must be understood in the context of Sparrow Faith as a gift from God, not as something due me. If I work forty hours per week for an employer, Sparrow Faith says that I am working as unto God not unto man. The money I receive from my employer is not my due from him, but rather is provision made available to me by grace as a gift from my Father who loves me. This fact then makes God my source of provision and my employer merely delegated by God as the current channel through which my provision comes.

Now with this understanding, if I hear that the company for which I work is downsizing and I may lose my employment, my heart is not terrorized by the fear of lack of provision, because my employer was not my source. The source has not changed. God's love for me has not changed. Therefore, my provision is secure. God may simply use a different channel through which to provide for my needs. Many people have thought that provision necessarily must be in the form of money. This is not true. God could provide for you a house, car, food, an airplane, whatever you need to fulfill your calling, all without money. Again, Mammon continually promotes the message that power for life is in money. God provided food for Elijah (1 Samuel 17), food, clothing and housing for Mephibosheth (2 Samuel 9), food for five thousand people through Jesus, all without money.

With this understanding, I become a manager of wealth and/or money, which comes to me as a gift by grace from my Heavenly Father. Recognizing that He is my source, money no longer controls my life. When the Lord speaks to me to give in an offering, I no longer see that as my money, which I worked hard to get—the purchasing power of which I am now relinquishing at great sacrifice to myself. No! I see myself as a manager of a small portion of God's resources over which He has made me manager. Because my personal provision is already secure in His love, it is not jeopardized when He asks me to direct some of His resource to a particular purpose in His Kingdom. I am no longer bound to pray to my checkbook when an offering opportunity is made available ("Oh, dear checkbook, how much is in you?"), but rather I am free to pray to the Living God to find out what He wants done with His resource.

Once again, Sparrow Faith is a key foundational principle. When this is not in place in a Christian's life, he will not see money as a tool with which to serve God, but rather he will only see the purchasing power of the money in exchange for goods and services which he needs. Let me give you a couple of practical examples.

I was ministering one time in Africa among native people. Most of these people considered themselves very poor. Some were not really so poor and had quite good jobs by the standards of the economy of that particular nation. I was ministering at a leadership conference for one week. The founder of this movement of churches took an offering at each meeting of the conference. Over the course of the week, a total offering in the equivalent of approximately forty-two U.S. dollars was received. The conference had cost him in direct expenses more than five times this to conduct. The church leaders attending the conference apparently saw no value in giving.

However, I had brought with me a selection of books and tapes, which I was prepared to give to these leaders. I realized, however, that they probably would not value these materials if I gave them at no cost. Therefore, I designated a nominal cost for each book or tape series. All of these materials were instantly purchased within the first two meetings. Now, it was interesting to note that these "poor" Christian leaders had no money to give in the offering, but plenty of money to buy what they desired. In other words, they did not recognize any value coming to them through giving in an offering, but recognized the immediate value of exchanging money for a book or tape series. This again is a strong symptom of bondage to the spirit of Mammon. Money only has value when it can be exchanged for something of immediate value. This attitude is not unique to rural Africa, but is also commonly found among Christians in any western country.

I remember seeing a survey done by Christian Retailers Magazine back in 1990 regarding the usage of money among Charismatic Christians worldwide. This survey found that the average Charismatic Christian gave into the Kingdom

$15.60 per year, or about $0.30 per week. However, the same group was found to spend $1.87 per week on Christian books, videos, cassettes, gifts, and conventions. Apparently, Charismatic Christians worldwide find far more value in purchasing "Christian stuff" than they do in giving toward the preaching of the gospel.

chapter 6
KNOW YOUR PLACE OF PROVISION

I was teaching this concept of "Sparrow Faith" in one meeting and a man posed the following question, "Are you saying then that if I believe that God is my source He will just automatically by His grace make provision for me?"

"Yes," I replied.

"If this is so, then I can just quit my job and expect God to provide for me, right?"

He was obviously being facetious to make a point. We would all recognize that there is something wrong with this thinking, but what is it?

The Lord led me to answer this man's question through a look at the life of Elijah in 1 Kings chapter 17. I discovered that it is important to recognize the place and channel through which God is making provision. In the case of the man who asked the question, God's channel of provision for him was through his present employment. I believe that many Christians have been confused because they have missed God's place and channel of provision.

Let us look at this account of Elijah's life.

1 KINGS 17

2   Then the word of the Lord came to him, saying,

3   'Get away from here and turn eastward, and hide by the Brook Cherith, which flows into the Jordan.

4   And it will be that you shall drink from the brook, and I have commanded the ravens to feed you there.'

5   So he went and did according to the word of the Lord, for he went and stayed by the Brook Cherith, which flows into the Jordan.

6   The ravens brought him bread and meat in the morning and bread and meat in the evening; and he drank from the brook. (NKJV)

The first point we see in the life of Elijah is that the word of the Lord came to him. Elijah received specific instruction form the Lord about his place of provision. He was not an atheist looking to money to be a source for him. He was listening to the spirit of God. This same principle is true for us. We need to be in dynamic relationship with the living God in order to know where our place of provision is. Many times in the life of most Christians, God will change the place and channel of provision. It is critical at these times to be listening to the spirit of God to know that the channel or place of provision has changed. Elijah heard from God that although there was a drought and famine in the land, he was to go to the Brook Cherith and ravens would there provide for him bread and meat.

I have noticed that in the lives of many Christians there is a tendency for great fear to come upon them at the times of provision channel changes. I believe that it is important for us to know that the channel and place of provision will change for most of us many times in our lives, but the source of provision remains the same.

Elijah acted on the word he had received from the Lord and moved from where he was to the Brook Cherith. God had not promised him money, only provision. Elijah could have remained where he was, experienced lack of provision, and become angry and bitter at God because of the lack. I believe that this happens to many Christians. They simply fail to recognize location and channel changes made by God in their provision. As a result, they find themselves in some place other than the place designated by God for their current provision.

Usually in order to recognize provision channel changes, it is necessary to have some prior relationship and experience with the Lord. It took some faith in God for Elijah to move from where he was to the brook. I am sure it took faith to believe that ravens would really bring him food daily. It must have taken faith to eat the meat and bread that the ravens brought. Have you ever thought about where ravens get bread and meat?

Let us look a little farther in the story.

1 KINGS 17

7 *And it happened after a while that the brook dried up, because there had been no rain in the land.*

8 *Then the word of the Lord came to him, saying,*

9 *'Arise, go to Zerepath, which belongs to Sidon, and dwell there, See, I have commanded a widow there to provide for you.' (NKJV)*

31

By the time the water in the brook dried up, Elijah had probably already learned that termination of provision through a particular channel is indicative of a channel change being made by God. Sure enough, the word of the Lord very quickly followed the drying up of the brook. Most Christians are thrown into a panic every time a particular channel that God has been using for provision dries up. Most people at these times are gripped by the spirit of Mammon and instantly become atheists. They begin frantically striving in their own strength to solve their provision problem. Sparrow Faith, on the other hand, does not abandon the source of provision, but simply recognizes a channel change.

If the man who asked me this question had simply quit his job and expected God to provide for him in the name of "Sparrow Faith", he would have found himself out of God's place of current provision for his life. It is critical to recognize the location and channel of your current provision from God.

I have always thought that another strange part of the instruction that Elijah received from the Lord was that he was to find a widow in Zerepath, and that she would be his next channel of provision. If I were Elijah, I would have thought that the Lord would send me to a rich person in Zerepath, not to a widow who did not even have enough provision for herself, let alone for a guest. As I meditated on this passage, I began to see that the Lord had a double purpose in this instruction. He was going to accomplish something in the life of the widow as well as make provision for Elijah. Let us read further.

1 KINGS 17

10 So he arose and went to Zerepath. And when he came to the gate of the city, indeed a widow was there gathering sticks. And he called to her and said, 'Please bring me a little water in a cup, that I may drink.'

11 And as she was going to get it, he called to her and said, 'Please, bring me a morsel of bread in your hand.'

12 So she said, 'As the Lord your God lives, I do not have bread, only a handful of flour in a bin, and a little oil in a jar; and see, I am gathering a couple of sticks that I may go in and prepare it for myself and my son, that we may eat it, and die.'

13 And Elijah said to her, 'Do not fear; go and do as you have said, but make me a small cake from it first, and bring it to me; and afterward make some for yourself and your son.'

14 For thus says the Lord God of Israel; 'The bin of flour shall not be used up, nor shall the jar of oil run dry, until the day the Lord sends rain on the earth.'

15 So she went away and did according to the word of Elijah; and she and he and her household ate for many days.

16 The bin of flour was not used up nor did the jar of oil run dry, according to the word of the Lord which He spoke by Elijah. (NKJV)

Again, this must have taken faith for Elijah to obey the word of the Lord. Can you imagine what it must have been like for Elijah to have to ask a destitute widow to prepare

33

food and drink for him? First of all, this would be extremely humbling. Secondly, it would offend one's own natural mind. If I were Elijah, I would have been thinking, "Lord, I must have missed your instruction. This widow is destitute. I should not be asking her to provide for me. I should be taking an offering amongst the rest of the town for her so that she can live. She says that she is so poor that she is preparing her last meal for her son and herself. Lord, there must be some mistake. I can't ask her to give to me." How terrible would you feel to have to do what God asked Elijah to do?

Can you imagine meeting a destitute widow who is preparing her last bit of food before she dies, and the Lord tells you to tell her, "Before you prepare that meal, first get me a drink of water and prepare me a small cake and bring it to me". (1 Kings 17:12-13)

Why did the Lord have Elijah ask this woman to give him her last little bit of food? I believe that again the issue in this woman's life was Sparrow Faith. In what was she trusting for provision? I believe it is evident that she was trusting in her supply of flour and oil. Since these had run out, she was now expecting to die. God wanted to move her faith from the material provision to the living God. He wanted to be her source of provision. How did He choose to accomplish this? He had the man of God ask her to give him her last bit of material provision. This removed her ability to trust in the flour and oil for sustenance.

Neither God, nor Elijah was after her flour and oil. God was after her faith. He wanted to be her source. I believe that many times this same thing is true regarding men of God receiving offerings today. Some people feel that they are after the money. Not all have right motives, but I believe that most of the time the man of God is not after people's money. He and God are after their faith. Faith in God releases miracles.

When the widow did what Elijah asked her to do, she released a supernatural miracle of God. The oil and flour did not run out for many days. She learned to live by trusting the word of the Lord instead of material possessions.

I remember the first time I was asked by the Lord to do something similar to what Elijah had to do in this account. Several years ago, I worked full time in a Christian counseling ministry. This ministry was supported by the donations of those who came for ministry. As counselors, we asked each person to whom we ministered to pray at the end of each session and ask the Lord what they were to give as an offering that day.

After ministering to one young man, I asked him to pray about what to give as an offering that day. He responded that we did not even need to pray, as he was destitute and had absolutely nothing to give. In my natural mind, I wanted to give to him. However, I felt the spirit of God rise up in me and I found myself saying to him, "I don't believe you. Show me your wallet." He opened his wallet, and sure enough, he had nothing.

I then said to him "I know you have something to give. Empty your pockets." He did, and out came fifty cents. "I knew you had something!" I said.

I watched terror strike his face as he said, "That fifty cents is all I have, and I need all of it to get home on the bus. I got these fifty cents by returning soda pop bottles to the grocery store. It's snowing outside. I live sixteen miles away from here and it costs fifty cents to get home on the bus. I need the whole fifty cents for bus fare."

My heart went out to this man, but I also realized that his trust was in his fifty cents, not in God. Mammon had him bound in fear and love of money. Neither God nor I were after his money. We were both after his faith. He was a practical atheist. God was not in his thinking of how he would get home.

I told him, "Since the bus costs fifty cents, if you give then you place yourself in the position of being a candidate for a miracle. We are going to pray to ask the Lord how much of the fifty cents you are to give in the offering this afternoon. You have to know that I am not interested in your money. You could give the entire fifty cents and it wouldn't really make a great deal of difference to this ministry."

I felt a little badly for this fellow, as I had to speak quite sternly to him. It seemed a bit strange to take the last fifty cents from an indigent man who had nothing. However, I knew that if I did not press this point with him, he would never be free of the spirit of Mammon, who had kept him in poverty through his trust in money for a long time. He finally agreed and we prayed. He felt that he was to give five cents. I made change for him, and we then prayed over his five-cent offering. He renounced his trust in money, declared his independence from the spirit of Mammon, and his reliance upon the Lord Jesus Christ as his source of provision.

This man then went out of my office, still grumbling about how he was now going to have to walk home sixteen miles in the snow, because he didn't have enough money for the bus fare. Next week when he returned, this man had, as you might suspect, a great miracle story. He told me that when he arrived at the bus stop, still angry, he looked down and there at the base of the bus stop sign was a nickel. He picked it up and thought to himself, "Boy, that sure was lucky". He said it didn't even dawn on him until he was half way home that the nickel he "happened" to find was the provision of the Lord for his ride home. When he got home, he then found an unexpected check in the mail for five dollars. He considered this a one hundred-fold return on his offering of five cents.

When the man came for his appointment the next week, he was so excited about the offering, he could hardly wait for the counseling session to be over so he could give in the offering and exercise his faith in God as his source again. I cannot remember exactly, but he had something like a total of two dollars to pray about that second week. This man grew in faith and finances week by week. The five-cent offering I received from him turned out to be the key that broke his trust in money and began to prove to him God's faithfulness as a source of provision.

chapter 7
LIVING ON THE THIRD RIVER

Have you ever thought about funding Kingdom work from God's perspective? God has an infinite supply of resource. However, we usually see that churches and ministries doing Kingdom work have a very limited and usually scarce supply of resource. Why? Does God not want to supply? No, this is not the problem. How does resource get from God's supply into the hands of the end-user ministries? This happens primarily through people. Each Christian is like a pipeline through which God desires to flow financial resource into the Kingdom. However, many of the pipelines are extremely clogged and leaky. Most of what God puts down the pipe never makes it out the other end.

If Sparrow Faith is not established, fear causes most of the resource to be collected in the pipeline. If there is massive debt then much of the resource is siphoned out of the pipeline in the form of interest. If there is not a fixed budget for personal consumption, then most of the resource is consumed on making a bigger, better and more comfortable pipe. This must be very frustrating for the Lord.

Do you remember the parable we started with regarding the three rivers? Now suppose that you are the person in the snowfield who decides how much water to release into each river. Which river would you put most of the water down? I would put most of the water down river number 3. How much are you going to release into river number 1? I would probably put enough down this river to meet the need of that man who lives down there because I love him, and want him to be taken care of. However, there is no use for that water making a large lake on his property. It just becomes stagnant, like a Dead Sea. I would just put enough water down there for that family to use.

How much water would you put in the second river? I would probably send only enough water to meet the need of the people who live along that river. There is no point in sending huge quantities of water down this river, as it will be improperly used. The majority of water will of course be sent down the third river, so that it will be utilized to bring the most benefit to the greatest number of people.

We have found that many times non-Christians have a better sense of living along the third river than do Christians. We have found unbelievers who have learned to live with a closed circle budget and are really already living along the third river, while their Christian neighbors are still living along the first or second rivers believing God for "the wealth of the wicked to be transferred to the righteous." I believe that from God's perspective, it may be easier to bring the unbeliever living on the third river into the Kingdom than to get the Christian living on the first or second river to shift paradigms to live on the third river. This may surprise many Christians as God builds His Kingdom in this new millennium. The sons of darkness sometimes exercise more wisdom than the sons of light.

In reality, whatever water is flowing down your river right now is probably about the amount that God finds you faithful to manage. If you desire to manage a greater portion of God's resources as a steward, this will require that you allow God to change you significantly on the inside. You will first need to learn to be faithful over what you have been given to manage now. The Lord can then bring about the necessary change in your thinking and perceptions of life to be able to understand how to manage greater amounts of resources in His Kingdom.

When I have learned how to live along the third river with the resources that I now have, I qualify myself to receive more of God's resources to channel into His Kingdom. The faster I can learn to build canals and channel resources into the Kingdom the faster I qualify myself to handle more resources. I believe that the Lord is simply looking for people with a credible track record, not people who are merely full of good intentions for the future. "When I have more money, I will give thus and such," they say, as they continue to mismanage what they have now. For many of us, this major paradigm shift will have to take place now in order to qualify us for the plan God has for us for the future.

Along which river are you now living? Along which river do you desire to live? Each of us must personally answer these questions before the Lord. Most people find that they are in reality living along the first or second river. If you desire to move to live along the third river, this will probably require a major paradigm shift. **People who live on the third river give and invest first, and spend what is left. People on the first and second rivers spend first and give and invest what is left.** If you truly desire to move to live along the third river, you will need to establish

Sparrow Faith in your heart. Then out of the security of knowing your needs are met because God loves you, you can begin to channel the water that God has sent down your river into the Kingdom.

If you can see that you have been living on the first or second river and would desire to move to live on the third river, a first step toward that goal may be to pray the following prayer.

Heavenly Father, thank You that You are totally faithful to provide for us (me) because You love us (me). Again, we (I) renounce the spirit of Mammon and any influence we (I) have allowed it to have in our (my) lives (life). We (I) ask You to give us (me) a deep knowing inside of the reality of Sparrow Faith. We (I) desire to live along the Third River and to qualify ourselves (myself) to manage greater amounts of Your resources. Forgive us (me) for the mismanagement of the past. Forgive us (me) for working for money, instead of directing money to work for us (me) to accomplish Your Kingdom purpose. We (I) now ask You for the grace and wisdom to begin to live on the Third River and to be manager(s) of Your resources. Lord Jesus, we (I) trust You to show us (me) into what areas of Your Kingdom we (I) are to begin to give the resources You have committed to flow through our (my) river and to increase the flow as we (I) are faithful. Amen

For a more in-depth study in the area of finances, read *Wealth, Riches & Money* co-authored by Craig Hill and Earl Pitts. A preview of PART ONE follows:

PART ONE:
BALANCE IN FINANCIAL WISDOM

In beginning a discussion on personal financial management, we had to ask the question, "Does God have anything to say about money in the Bible?" Many people consider the Bible to be a book pertaining to spirituality, but not to such mundane matters as personal management of money. As we began to study this topic in the Bible, we were amazed to discover that the New Testament contains nearly ten times as many verses regarding money and finances as it does salvation and faith. **The New Testament actually contains 215 verses pertaining to faith, 218 verses pertaining to salvation, and 2084 verses dealing with the stewardship of and accountability for money and finance.** Sixteen of Jesus' thirty-eight parables deal with money.

The question comes to mind, "Why?" Was Jesus a money-grabber? Did He come to earth to collect money to support His ministry? No, of course not! Jesus was not after people's money; He was after their hearts. He told us in Matthew 6:21, *"where your treasure is there shall your heart be also"*. Jesus simply found that many people considered their money a great treasure. He found that if He could capture their money, He could capture their hearts. We believe that the same is true today. Jesus is not after your money. He is after your heart. How we relate to money is simply indicative of the condition of our hearts.

Consequently, God has much to say to us about

finances, and He has given us His Word to instruct us. In order for us to carry out world evangelism, it is going to take hundreds of millions of dollars. In fact, I (Earl) have heard an estimate of two and a half billion US dollars being needed to preach the Gospel throughout the whole world. Christians are waiting for Jesus to return to earth. Some were expecting the end of the world at the turn of the millennium. However, the Word is very clear about when this will happen. Jesus, Himself, told us that when the Gospel of the Kingdom is preached as a witness to every people group, every ethnos, every nation, then the end shall come (Matthew 24:14). Perhaps this is similar to the instruction a primary school teacher might have given us as children when we had to remain at school in order to complete an unfinished assignment. "When you are finished with your assignment, you may go home." Many want to go home without finishing the assignment. The mandate, of course, is for us to go and preach the Gospel in the whole world. It is going to take finances to accomplish this task.

When we have finances, we can force the world system to do the work of the Kingdom of God. With finances we can buy television time and airplane tickets. We can print Bibles. We can go, preach, and make disciples. We can proclaim the Gospel of Jesus Christ. God has left us in the world after we were born again, in order to tell others about Jesus. He did not take us immediately to heaven. His plan is to have a vast family of men and women, boys and girls, of every tongue, every tribe, and every nation with whom He will spend eternity. He left us here and said, *"Go and preach My Gospel"* (paraphrase of Mark 16:15). It is going to take many people and much resource, which includes money, in order for that to take place.

One woman involved in full-time Christian ministry was

confronted about receiving money for the ministry. She was told, "You should not be requesting money from people who are receiving your Bible teaching. Jesus said the gospel is freely given. *'Freely you have received, freely give.'* (Matthew 10:8)." This wise Christian leader responded by saying, "Obviously you have never tried to take the gospel to anyone. We have not yet convinced the airlines, television stations, print shops and car dealerships that the Master has need of their resources, and they should freely give of their goods and services to be used in proclaiming the gospel."

When we talk about finances, it is important to distinguish between the management of personal finances and corporate finances. The scope of this book is limited to dealing with personal finances. Managing corporate or business finance in the Kingdom of God is another highly important topic to be addressed, but will not be covered in the present work. The first step toward managing a Kingdom-oriented business is to bring our personal finances into biblical order.

I (Earl) ran across a recent statistic citing the fact that 80 % of North American Christian homes have some type of financial distress, ranging from mild to serious. A primary issue cited in 50% of divorces in America today has to do with finances. Relationships have broken because of the mismanagement of finances, the lack of agreement over the usage of finances, or the mishandling of debt. In reality, the life of every single person is greatly impacted by his or her relationship to finances.

SPIRIT AND TRUTH

When Jesus was talking to the woman at the well in John chapter 4, He told her, *"God is Spirit, and those who worship Him must worship in spirit and truth"*. In everything we do, it is essential that we keep a balance between spirit and truth. Everything we do as believers should be a part of our worship unto God. Thus, as we enter into discussion about our relationship to money and finances, we want to endeavor throughout this book to keep a continual balance between spirit and truth. What do we mean by this?

The truth side primarily has to do with natural, non-optional principles of life, while the spirit side has to do with relating to the spirit realm. We need to constantly live in compliance with both spirit and truth. For example, understanding and obeying the principle of gravity would pertain to the truth side. One would create many problems for oneself in life if he/she did not understand or refused to abide by the principle of gravity.

Here is another example: when flying an airplane, one should understand and abide by the principles of aerodynamics. Violation of these principles can readily result in death or serious injury. However, one would also want to be led by the Holy Spirit regarding where and when to fly an airplane. It would be equally dangerous, while flying, either to violate a basic aerodynamic principle or to miss the specific direction of the Holy Spirit. This same balance is essential to be kept when dealing with personal finances.

On both the spirit and the truth side of the balance, we want to operate in faith. All that we do must be done in faith. Apostle Paul tells us in Romans 14:23 that *"whatever is not of faith is sin."* So, how do we walk in faith regarding basic financial principles (the truth side)? We find a key to this in a parable Jesus told his disciples in Luke 17. Jesus shared this parable in response to His disciples' request to increase their faith.

LUKE 17

6 *So the Lord said, "If you have faith as a mustard seed, you can say to this mulberry tree, 'Be pulled up by the roots and be planted in the sea,' and it would obey you.*

7 *And which of you having a servant plowing or tending sheep, will say to him when he has come in from the field, 'Come at once and sit down to eat?'*

8 *But will he not rather say to him, 'Prepare something for my supper, and gird yourself and serve me till I have eaten and drunk, and afterward you will eat and drink?'*

9 *Does he thank that servant because he did the things that were commanded him? I think not.*

10 *So likewise you, when you have done all those things which you are commanded, say, 'We are unprofitable servants. We have done what was our duty to do.'" (NKJV)*

At first glance, many people will look at this and wonder, "What on earth does this have to do with faith?" First, faith needs to be seen as a seed. The apostles wanted increase in their faith. A seed is for planting, so increase will come as it grows. As we abide in God's Word, live in it, let it mold our thinking, faith will grow and develop in our hearts. Jesus is telling His disciples here that faith comes through obedience and accountability. Faith is increased when a servant simply does that which he is told to do.

Faith comes through recognizing our position as servants, and through becoming obedient to the Master's instructions already given to us in the Word of God.

On the one hand, we find many people who believe God for financial increase and multiplication, but are regularly violating biblical financial principles. You may be a mighty man or woman of faith, but it would still be unwise for you to violate the law of gravity by stepping off tall cliffs and buildings. In the financial realm, you cannot regularly violate basic, financial principles and expect that by "faith" God will bring deliverance, increase, and multiplication. Faith, on the truth side, comes through obedience to basic life principles.

In the chart on page 10, you will see listed on the truth side seven basic financial building blocks. These basic principles are similar to the law of gravity and cannot be violated without consequence. Violation results in turmoil, stress, financial pressure, poverty, and often disaster. Obedience as a servant to these basic instructions will build faith, and produce security, peace, and prosperity.

Through the course of this book, we will examine in more detail each of these seven basic principles pertaining to the management of personal finances. We will see that these building blocks must be put in place sequentially. Many Christians have become angry with God or with Bible teachers by attempting to operate in the principles of sowing and reaping (Building Block #7) when they have not yet established in their lives Building Blocks one through six. Such people then feel either deceived by Bible teachers or abandoned by God. In most cases, neither is true. These people have simply attempted to build a financial house with no foundation or frame structure. Many people are looking for a "quick fix" to their financial problems rather then being willing to first build a strong foundation and frame structure.

On the other hand, some have focused only on the truth side of the equation. Such people concentrate only on principles of sound financial management. However, one must also be attentive to the spirit side of the equation. We have found many people who understand correct biblical principles of financial management, but seem to have an inability to practically implement that which they know. Often this is due to a lack of understanding of the spirit side of the equation. There is a literal battle that is taking place in the spirit realm over our lives and financial decisions (Ephesians 6:12).

I (Craig) perceive the spirit realm to be likened to the realm in which television waves operate. Probably in the place in which you now are reading this, TV waves are present. You have no perceptive apparatus by which you could see the picture or hear the sound. However, just because you cannot perceive television waves does not mean that they do not exist. Television waves are not just a concept or an idea, but rather are a physical reality.

This is how it is in the spirit realm. You may have little perceptive ability to experience the spirit realm in which God, angels, demons, and Satan operate. However, this does not mean that these spirit beings do not exist, or that they do not influence your life. They most certainly do, and it would behoove you to become aware of their influence upon your life and circumstances, if you are not already so aware. These influences hinder many people from being able to practically implement the truth they know.

On the spirit side of the equation, we also want to

recognize that it is important to be led by the Holy Spirit in all that we do financially. For example, we may recognize the basic principle of managing our finances through a budget. However, we also want to be led by the Holy Spirit as to what items are to be included in that budget. God really does have an opinion on everything pertaining to our lives. We may recognize basic principles of giving, saving or investing. Again we want to be led specifically by the Holy Spirit in the when, where, why, and how much pertaining to our giving, saving, and investing. Being led by the Holy Spirit can make a tremendous difference in the financial outcome of such activities.

In considering the spirit side of the equation, again we want to operate in faith. Apostle Paul tells us in Romans 10:17 (NKJV), *"So then faith comes by hearing and hearing by the Word of God".* There are two Greek words translated in English as 'word.' 'Logos' is used when the written word or collective sayings of God are being referred to. The second Greek word is 'rhema' which refers to the spoken word: God speaking His Word to our hearts; the voice of the Spirit putting emphasis on His written Word; God speaking His Word to our spirit. When this happens the potential for faith to arise in our hearts takes place. When we meditate on the Word of God (logos), and hearing God speak His Word (rhema), faith comes! (By the way, faith in someone else comes when we hear someone else's word and receive it.) Thus as we meditate upon specific promises that God has given us in His Word and allow God to confirm this Word to us, faith arises in our hearts toward God for the fulfillment of these promises in our lives.

In looking at the chart on page 10, we can see that on the spirit side we must recognize that everything we have comes to us as a gift from God. Anything you have ever received in your life from God, you received by His grace. Nothing came to you because of your works. All through life, there is always a tension between relating to God based on human works as opposed to relating to Him based on His grace. Most people need to make a major paradigm shift in the area of receiving provision as a gift from God by His grace, rather than as something deserved or earned. We will have much more to say about this in a later section.

We see in 2 Corinthians 9:8 that God _is able_ to make all _grace abound._ He is not obligated. He is able. He does so because He loves us, but not because He has to.

When we combine both aspects of spirit and truth, we see that faith will be developed in us both through hearing and through meditating on the Word of God and through obedience to establish the basic building blocks in our lives. As we do our part to establish these building blocks and receive God's grace, then God does His part in making all grace come to us in abundance to meet every need!

Let us now look at the following chart that outlines this balance between spirit and truth.

JOHN 4:23-24

SPIRIT   TRUTH

Faith *Romans 10:17* **Word** **GRACE**	**Faith** *Luke 17:5-10* **Obedience** **BUILDING BLOCKS**
2 CORINTHIANS 9:8 *And God is able to make all grace (every favor and earthly blessing) come to you in abundance, so that you may always and under all circumstances and whatever the need, be self sufficient, possessing enough to require no aid or support and furnished in abundance for every good work and charitable donation.* (Amplified)	**1. RECOGNIZE AND RENOUNCE THE SPIRIT OF MAMMON** (Heart allegiance goes to God alone) **2. ESTABLISH SPARROW FAITH** (God is my source) **3. ESTABLISH THE TITHE** (Be a tither rather than just tithing) **4. BECOME GOD'S MANAGER** (Become accountable to God for administration of present resources) **5. CLOSE THE CIRCLE** (How much is enough?) **6. STEP UP TO YOUR DEBT** (Acknowledge and properly deal with all debt) **7. BECOME A FINANCIAL EUNUCH** (Manage the overflow for the Lord)

⬅ HUMILITY

As we consider the above chart, we notice that we cross over from the truth side to the spirit side in humility. The reason we say this is that some people have viewed God as a computer or a machine. If they honor the principles, then they feel that they have a right to demand that God meet their need. No, God is not a machine. He is a person, and He should be related to in humility as we would relate to any other person. What father would like to have his children demand that he do thus and such because they had done what he said? No, it is His pleasure to provide for His children, but it hurts His heart to have His children demand that He perform. Thus, God is not <u>required</u> to do anything. He is a person and chooses to provide for us because He loves us.

As Jesus brought out in the parable in Luke 17, even after we have done everything required, we still have nothing with which to demand that God do anything. He is the master and we are the servants. The servant never comes to the master to demand anything, even when he has done all that the master required. Thus, even when we have adhered to all the truth-side principles, we still cross over onto the spirit side in humility as servants. We are not demanding anything of God, but rather we are receiving of His provision for us by His grace; we are managing the overflow He passes through us as administrators of His account, not possessors of our own accounts.

Through the course of this book, we will be looking at the seven foundational principles listed in the preceding chart. Each time we come to a new principle, we will repeat the chart, to remember to always keep the balance between spirit and truth. Let us now move on to talk about the spiritual power behind money and how it influences believers.

APPENDIX

ABOUT THE AUTHOR

Craig Hill and his wife, Jan, live near Denver, Colorado, U.S.A. Craig and Jan give senior leadership to Family Foundations International (FFI). FFI is a non-profit Christian ministry through which life-changing seminars are conducted in many nations of the world. Craig has written several books, including his best seller, *The Ancient Paths*.

Through his past experience in business, missions, counseling and pastoral ministry, God has given Craig unique insight into marriage, family, financial and interpersonal relationships. This has resulted in his ability to identify for many people, root causes of relational conflict, compulsive habits, low self-esteem, workaholism, lack of financial provision and other undesirable life patterns, which are repeated from one generation to the next.

By interweaving personal stories with biblical truths, God has anointed Craig to pierce through the veil of the mind to minister to the depths of the heart, resulting in authentic life change for many.

SEMINARS & COURSES

www.familyfoundations.com

Family Foundations International

*Embracing God's Ancient Paths of Blessing–
An Experience of the Heart You'll Never Forget!*

Family Foundations (FFI) is a non-profit Christian ministry, based out of Colorado, USA. FFI provides seminars and other tools through local churches and businesses in many countries around the world. Craig & Jan Hill are the founders of FFI.

The Ancient Paths Experiences give solid biblical principles, and Craig Hill's moving examples open the heart for participants to receive truth and rest for their souls. The intent of the teaching is not just for information, but to touch the heart. This often exposes hidden areas of woundedness that have occurred in the participant's life. The small group times allow participants to seek and receive God's powerful truth and light in these areas.

For a schedule of seminars or to locate the FFI office nearest you, please visit www.familyfoundations.com. Seminars are available through FFI Seminar Coordinators. Courses are available for purchase.

SEMINARS

An Ancient Paths Experience: EMPOWERING RELATIONSHIPS

Empowering Relationships is a teaching and small group seminar highlighting life's relationships with God, self and others. This 12-hour seminar includes the following topics:

- Relational versus Topical Communication
- Winning the Battle Over Destructive Attitudes, Habits and Behavior
- Removing Roots That Damage or Destroy Relationships
- Understanding and Breaking Eight Negative Adult Life Patterns

An Ancient Paths Experience: BLESSING GENERATIONS

Blessing Generations is a teaching and small group seminar on the power of blessing in seven critical times in life. In this 12-hour seminar, participants learn and experience the power of the blessing as the single most important factor that empowers people to prosper. Come, learn and apply the blessing in your life. Topics include

- Seven Critical Times of Blessing in Our Lives
- Consequences of the Lack of Blessing
- Impartation of the Father's Blessing
- The Power Behind Your Name

THE ANCIENT PATHS EXPERIENCE

The Ancient Paths Experience is the original 16-hour seminar including the topics of both Empowering Relationships and Blessing Generations Experiences in a condensed format.

An Ancient Paths Experience: COVENANT MARRIAGE (Covenant Marriage Retreat)

Married couples come to understand God's heart for their marriage, the true meaning of covenant and the power of a covenant commitment!

Learn how to add intimacy and unity as a couple and how to divorce-proof your marriage. The weekend ends in a covenant vows renewal ceremony where many couples realize for the first time the power of the covenant words in the vows they speak, sealing their marriage for life. Topics include:

- Communication in Marriage
- How to Divorce-Proof Your Marriage
- Understanding God's Heart, His Perfect Way, for Your Marriage
- Why the Biblical View On Blood Covenant and the Threshold Covenant Are Critical To Your Marriage
- How Marriage and Covenant Reflect the Image of God

An Ancient Paths Experience: OVERCOMING ANGER

Overcoming Anger is a seminar that presents practical, biblically-based reasons for anger and solutions to overcome anger and other compulsive habits in people's lives. Topics include:

- The Anger Cycle
- Why Do I Do What I Don't Want To Do?
- Identifying the Real Source of Anger and Frustration
- Removing the Power of People and Circumstances to Control My Life
- Three Key Steps to Overcoming Anger

An Ancient Paths Experience: TRANSFORMING HEARTS

This is a follow-up (level 2) seminar, which may be attended following any seminar with small group ministry. Topics include:

- The authority of the believer
- Freedom from shame
- Softening the hardened heart
- Refocus on who I am in Christ

An Ancient Paths Experience: FINANCIAL FOUNDATIONS

This seminar (and its predecessor named "Financial Success" is different from many Christian finance seminars. The teaching does not feature merely "practical" information on finances, but follows Craig Hill's anointed understanding of God's Word in teaching finances from a biblical and heart perspective (Matt. 6:21). Topics include:

- Discover the difference between wealth, riches and money
- What is "Mammon?"
- Learn a systemized guide to getting out of debt
- Learn five scriptural uses of money
- Learn how to release God's blessing in finances

An Ancient Paths Experience: THE QUESTION

This is an exciting and life-changing teaching and audio/video presentation designed especially for young men and young women, but found to open hearts of men and women of all ages. The Question (a 12-hour event) includes thought provoking teaching on video and small groups where the participants can share, and receive prayer and Holy Spirit-led ministry to the heart. There are two separate versions of The Question, one for women and one for men. The question is, "WHO AM I?" Topics include:

- Who Have I Allowed to Answer That Question For Me?
- What Difference do My Actions Today Make?
- How Should I Relate to the Opposite Gender?
- How Will I Know When I Meet The Right Person Who Is My Future Spouse?

Training for Ministry

FFI's Training is an intensive time of teaching leaders and potential leaders how to identify problems and allow the Holy Spirit to guide in effective prayer ministry through small groups. Prerequisite: You must have completed at least one Family Foundations Experience. Topics include:

- Authority and Leadership
- Philosophy of Ministry
- Process of Ministry
- Ministering to Shame
- Steps of Blessing
- Identifying Strongholds

COURSES

COMMUNICATION IN MARRIAGE: *Renewing the Bond of Love*

This eight-week course, which can be purchased and conducted at the local level, is intended for a small group of married couples with a leader couple. Topics include:

- Why women criticize/accuse, and men don't listen/care

- Why have we lost the feeling of romantic love and how can we regain it?

- Learn to identify and meet the five top priority desires of your spouse

- Emotional cycles and key differences in how men and women cope with stress

- Three steps necessary to solve arguments and resolve conflict

- Conquering the single greatest hindrance to fulfillment in marriage

COURTSHIP: *God's Ancient Path to Romance and Marriage*

Courtship is a 10-week video-based study in courtship versus dating for parents and teens. This material, which can be purchased and conducted at the local level, is designed for a small group (4-5 families) of parents and young people to join together to learn and work through the topic of courtship. The goal of the course is for parents and children to have a thorough understanding of the dangerous implications of dating (the world's system) in order to come into agreement about partnering for the identification of God's choice for the son/daughter's spouse. Topics include:

- God's Plan for Romance

- Courtship vs. Dating

- Standards for Relationships

- The Door to a Young Person's Heart

- Root Causes of Teenage Rebellion

- Eight character qualities to look for in a potential spouse

- Seven Phases of a Godly Courtship

FOR A FULL LISTING OF AVAILABLE RESOURCES AND COURSES AND A CURRENT SCHEDULE OF SEMINARS, PLEASE VISIT US AT

WWW.FAMILYFOUNDATIONS.COM

303.797.1139 PHONE

303.797.1579 FAX